# Calm Forest

# Native American Flute Songbook

*Calm Forest. Native American Flute Songbook* © 2015 by Wojciech Usarzewicz and FluteCraft

FIRST EDITION

ISBN: 978-83-64699-14-6


**PUBLISHER:**

FluteCraft
Website: http://flutecraft.org
Published in 2015, EU

Become a fan on FB:
http://facebook.com/flutecraftblog

If you wish to use these songs for commercial/non-commercial purposes, please use the original recordings available on **Jamendo.**

**https://www.jamendo.com/en/artist/473090/wojciech-usarzewicz**

# Table of Contents

# Introduction

If you're a beginner when it comes to Native American style flutes, this songbook will help you learn how to play this wonderful instrument. We'll start with basic scale and decorations, and then we progress to learning different songs.

Native American style flute is a woodwind instrument, usually made of wood, with five or six finger holes, a mouthpiece and a sound mechanism under the wooden block. Understanding how the instrument works isn't really necessary to play it. If you wish to use this songbook, all you need is a flute and some patience.

The best way to learn how to play Native American style flute is through practice. The instrument itself is one of the simplest flutes in the world to play – all you have to do is to learn the scale (the sounds which can be produced on your particular flute). It means you need to learn how to close and open finger holes in correct order. And you don't need to learn anything about music theory or even how to read notes.

This book contains tablature for songs that you can play on your Native American Flute. Instead of music notes, I use simple, explained tablature which allows you to play music right away! Tablature is a word that describes a graphical way to write down sounds on a specific instrument. In case of Native American flutes, tablature is a way to picture which finger holes must be open or closed to play a specific sound and create music as a result.

All the songs in this songbook were composed by me. Some of them are very simple to play, some are more complex. I composed them with teaching in mind. Some of the songs in this songbook can be heard on my album "Native American Flute Dreams Vol. 1", some can be heard on "Awakening" album.

## Will Your Flute Work?

If you own a Native American style flute with either five or six finger holes, you can play 99% of the songs from this songbook. Native American flutes come in different "keys". The key of the flute is the note which the flute plays when all the finger holes are closed. But it doesn't matter really what key you own.

The tablature from this book works for all possible keys of Native American style flutes. Oh, and what's with the "style"? Well, the US law prohibits non-native flute makers from using the term "Native American Flute", so instead they use "Native American style flute" term – it's a law thing that helps to tell a difference if the instrument has been built by a Native American, or just a craftsman. But beside that, there's no difference, it's still the same type of flute.

## What About Music Theory?

Music is written down with notes on a staff. The position of the note defines the pitch of the sound that must be played, and the shape of the note defines the length the sound must be played – this is the basic concept of written music. But you don't have to learn it at all, if you don't want to. All you need is the tablature, a graphical way to picture different notes. This is what you will learn soon. So don't worry, there's no need to learn music notation for the purpose of this book.

Also, if you ever wish to compose your own songs and write them down, you can use the tablature, as well. Again, no need to read normal notes.

# Learn to Play Native American Flute
# The Basics

First, you will learn the absolute basics for playing the Native Flute – just in case you never played this instrument before. In this chapter, you'll also learn how to read the graphical tablature.

## Your Flute

On the picture below, you can see a graphical representation of the Native American style flute. On the top, you see the blow hole. Below it, there's a block and the True Sound Hole. And down below, there are six (or five) finger holes. This is the universal way of picturing a typical Native Flute in many songbooks or on-line sources.

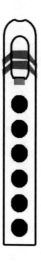

## Playing the Native American style Flute - the Basics

Playing the Native American style flute is not difficult. With few minutes of practice, you can already make simple melodies. Within an hour you can memorize a couple of songs, and after few weeks of regular practice you can play nicely your own songs. But before you do so, some fundamental and basic elements should be learned. Learning how to play the flute is possible with on-line resources. A face-to-face teacher is a great idea, but if you cannot find one (like I couldn't do so), the Internet is your friend.

Right now you will learn how to form an embouchure, how to blow into the flute, and how to make the sound. Then, you will learn how to play the scale and form basic melodies. And finally, you will learn how to read the simplest tablature for Native American flute music.

## Make the First Sound

An obvious thing to do when you wish to learn how to play the flute is to make the first sound. This requires learning how to form an embouchure with your mouth and how you breathe in the air into the mouthpiece, and of course, how to actually hold the flute. Before you do so, there are few things you need to learn.

- First, if you're a total beginner, the best way to hold the flute is the one that feels comfortable and allows you to seal the finger holes nicely. So just get comfortable.

- With time, you will notice that different flutes requires a different way to hold them. Small flutes are the easiest flutes to play. But the bigger the flute, the bigger the challenge. The bigger the flute, the heavier it becomes, so angle at which you hold the flute will change. Sometimes, you may need to hold the big bass flute almost vertically, because large flutes will weaken your muscles after a couple minutes of playing.

- Also, the bigger the flute, the bigger the space between finger holes become. If you have small hands, you may even be unable to play a bass flute. Most people can still hold and play an F#4 flute, but anything bigger than that may prove difficult. Keep this in mind when buying your first flute.

- Notice the angle between your fingers and the rest of the flute – it should not be a 90 degrees angle :). Thus do not place your fingers perpendicular to the flute's body. Rest them at an angle, say 60 to 50 degrees. This increases your accuracy, the seal of the finger holes, and the speed of your fingers. It becomes quite useful when you wish to learn flute decorations and articulations.

Take the flute into both your hands and place it in front of you at a general 45 angle, the end of the flute facing the ground – the bigger the flute, the more vertical your hold becomes. Notice – the fingers 2, 3 and 4 of both hands are used to cover the finger holes – the little fingers, but mainly the thumbs are used to support the flute. Make sure your back is straight, and that your diaphragm is free to operate. This will support your breathing.

Now lean the flute's mouthpiece on your lower lip, and cover the mouthpiece with your upper lift while not putting the mouthpiece into your mouth – this will form an embouchure with your mouth. And this may take a bit of practice... or not :). It depends on the flute – different flutes have different shapes of mouthpieces. Generally, what you want to do is the above, more or less – enclose the mouthpiece with your lips while not placing the flute in your mouth.

This way, you will get better control over the flow of the air and its pressure, and you will limit the amount of moisture getting into the flute.

The next step is to cover all the finger holes – depending on your flute, there may be five or six of them. Cover the finger holes with your flat fingers, and not with the tips of your fingers. Flat fingers provide a much better seal on the finger holes. If the seal is not complete, the flute will make a squeaky sound. Always make sure you seal the holes properly.

Now, blow the air into the flute. Do this gently at first, and start increasing the strength and pressure of the air flow bit by bit. As you do so, you will notice the sound getting from weak to loud, from "unsure" to steady. And in case of some flutes, you may even notice an overblown, when the tone of the flute's sound goes up significantly.

Notice the pressure you need to apply in order for your flute to produce a steady and clear sound. When all the finger holes are closed, the sound the flute makes is called "the fundamental" – it's the flute's fundamental tone, or "Key". There are different Keys – it's a term originating in the European music theory. Popular keys of the flute are A, G and F#, but don't worry about that. You should already know the Key of your own flute, it's usually marked on the flute, or written down in the flute's chart or the documentation of your flute.

## Pentatonic Scale Up and Down

It's time to learn to play the pentatonic scale on your flute. Your standard Native American style flute should have six holes. If it has five holes only, don't worry – this is normal, as well. Just ignore the forth hole which is usually closed when playing. Some makers create five holes flutes because they say it's more traditional. Most songs for the Native American style flute doesn't require six holes, and five holes will be enough.

**Learn now:**

- Black holes on the tablature are closed. You cover them with your fingers.

- White holes on the tablature are open. You leave them open.

Now, look at the image below. It's a scale of the flute that goes up and down. We call it "minor pentatonic scale". These are the basic sounds your flute can produce.

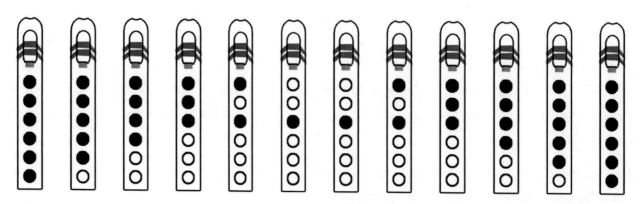

Play the scale up and down. Star slowly, and increase the speed. Practice this for a few days if necessary. The faster you play the scale, the better your "finger dexterity" becomes, which makes playing the flute easier over time.

## Improving Your Music

Many songs are "decorated" with ornaments such as grace note or thrill. You will learn these now.

### Grace Note

Grace note is a quick "jump" between two notes. It is usually played either with the 5th or 6th note being open for a short period of time. You play it between two notes that can be the same notes or different notes, and you make the jump quickly – it's just a decoration.

Grace notes are usually represented with a smaller image of a flute.

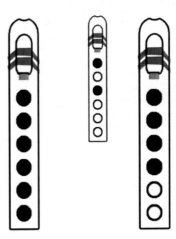

Based on the tablature on the right, you play the fundamental note for some time, then you quickly play the grace note, like 1/4 of second long, and then you play the 3rd note for some time.

Each grace note will be pictured as a smaller flute image between two different tablature notes.

### Thrill

Thrill is a rapid process of opening and closing a note hole. It is pictured with a thrill symbol above the tablature image.

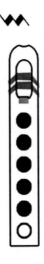

When you see it, you should rapidly play the note the following way:

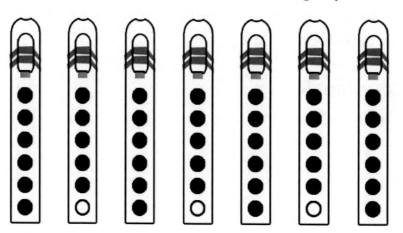

Play this rapidly.

## Pause

Whenever you see this image:

You can pause – this is a pause between parts of the song, like the silence between the phrases, or a dot at the end of a sentence.

## Speed of the Songs

Each of the songs in this book can be played with various speeds. Speed of playing the notes is usually defined with the picture of the note on the staff, or with digits written down below the note. For the purpose of this book, I decided to skip the speed thing all together.

I did so, because I believe the mood of your music, often shaped by the speed of playing the music, should be defined with you heart, and not with digits. That said, I include some introduction words for each of the songs, so you can learn whether the song is energetic or more contemplative etc. This should help you create your own style of playing the music from this book.

## Tips for learning:

- First play all the notes without decorations, and play them with the same speed.

- As you get better with the song, experiment with different speed – play some notes faster, and other notes slower. Find your own pace to create your own interpretation of the song.

- You can add your own decorations such as grace notes or thrills wherever you wish, even if it's not included in the tablature.

You can also follow the tablature note by note while listening to the free recording of the song (each song recording is linked) and follow my playing pace.

# Songbook

We start with something very simple – the following three songs are very short, but they will help you learn to play the flute while you're still a beginner. Then, we move through more complex and longer songs, up to songs from "Awakening" album, which are long and complex.

# Learning song 1

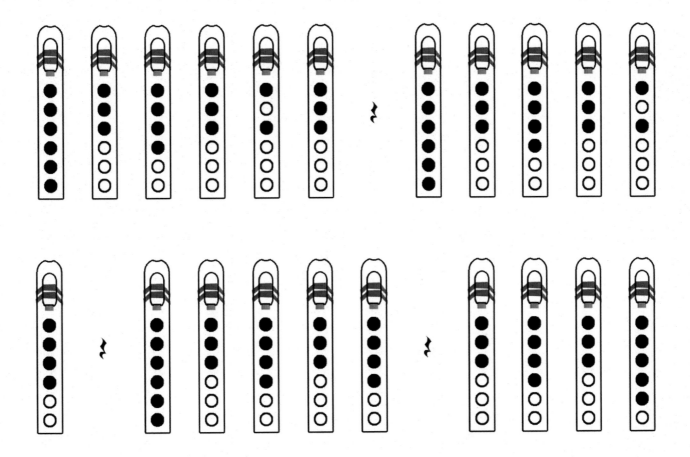

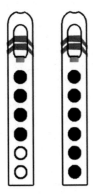

## Learning song 2

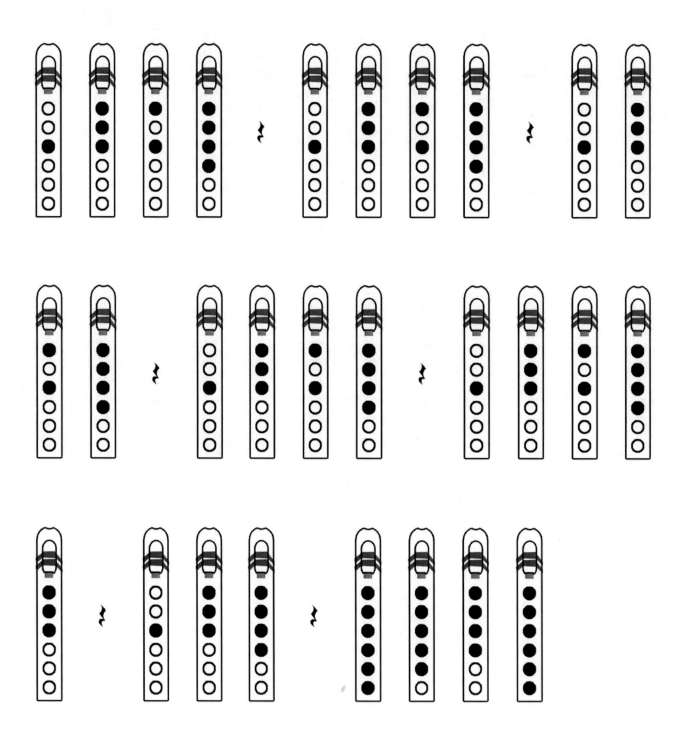

# Learning song 3

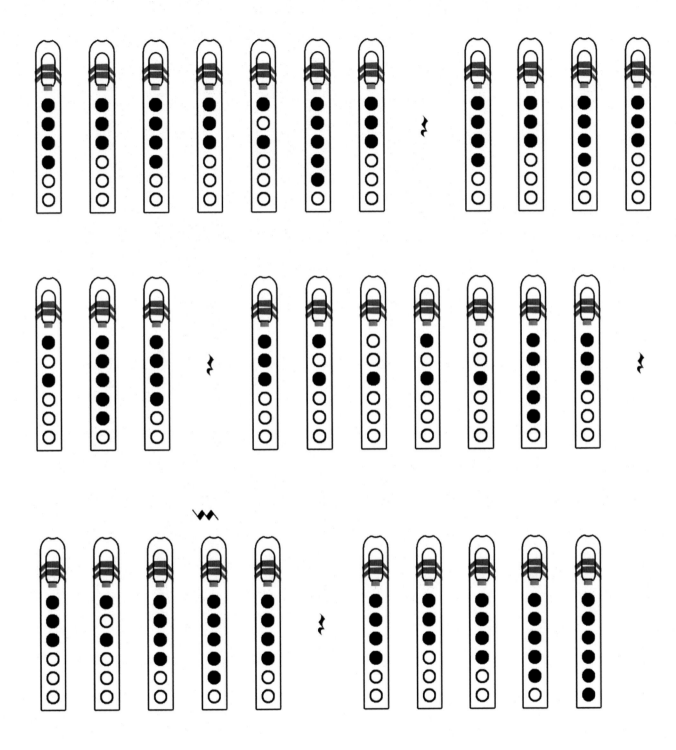

## Dreams

Listen for free: https://www.jamendo.com/track/1274486/dreams

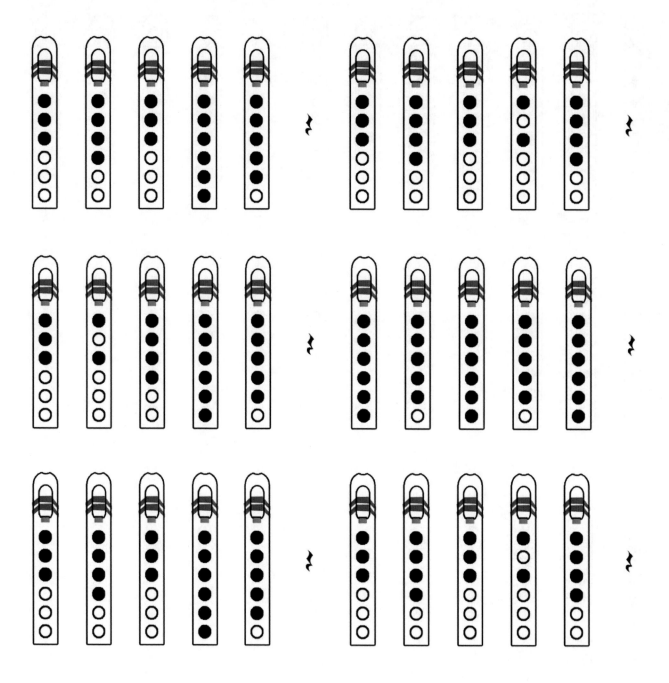

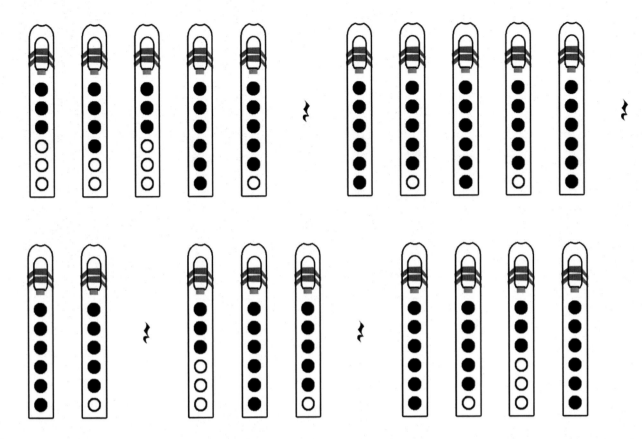

# Rain

Listen for free - https://www.jamendo.com/track/1274488/rain

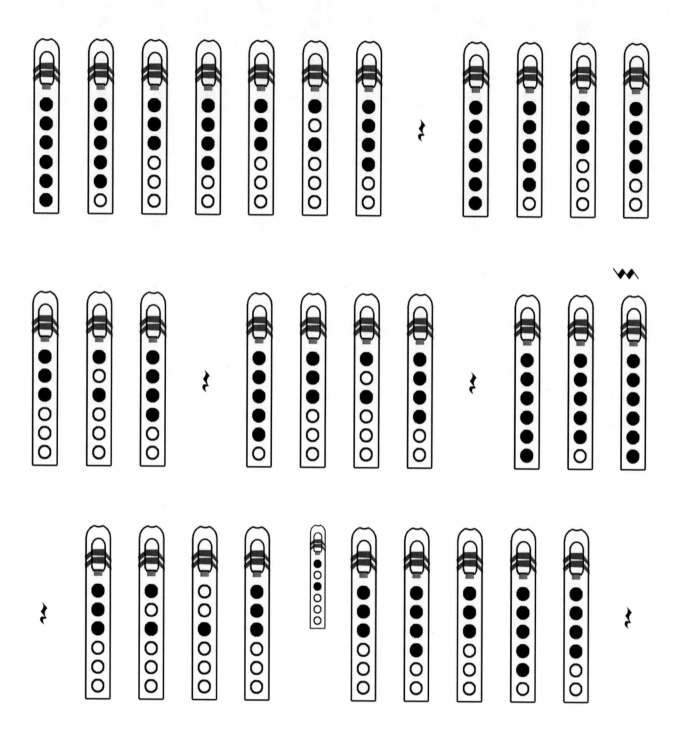

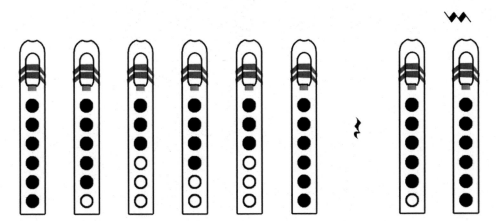

# Walking Through the Woods

Listen for free - https://www.jamendo.com/track/1274494/walking-through-the-woods

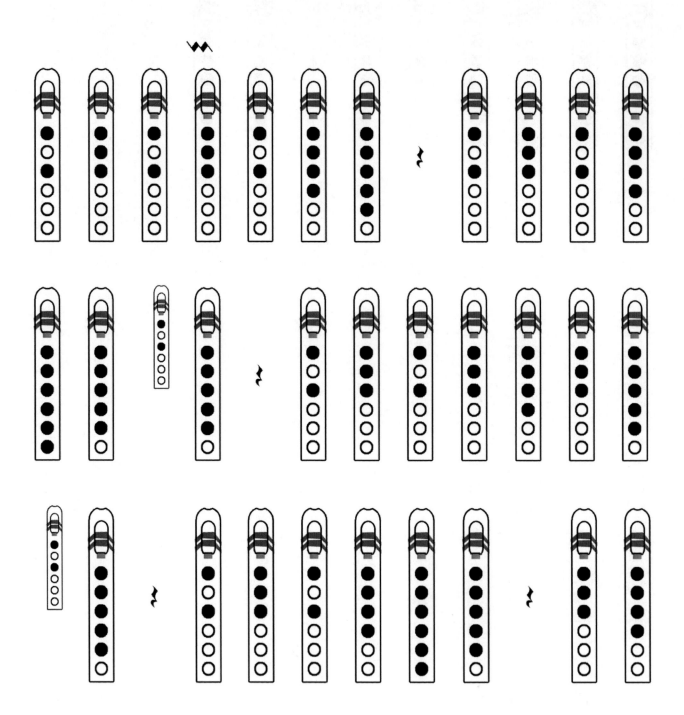

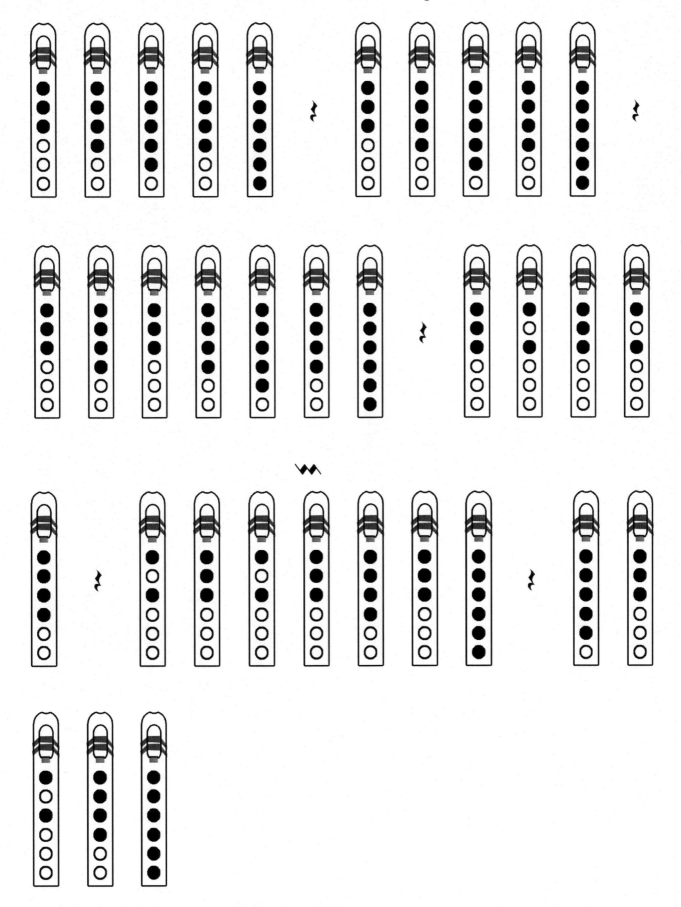

# Calm Forest

Listen for free - https://www.jamendo.com/track/1274487/calm-forest

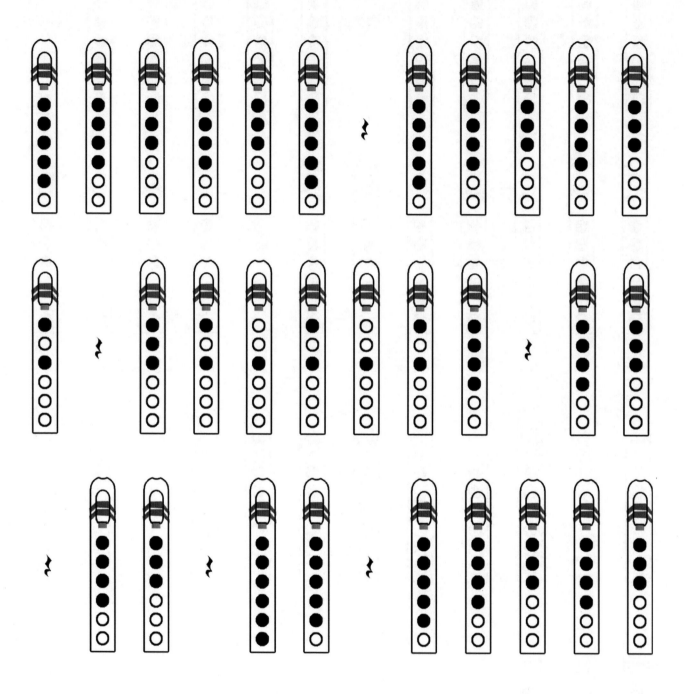

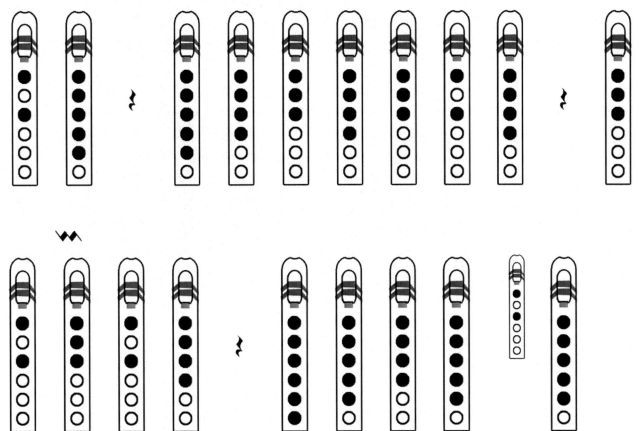

## Stories

Listen for free - https://www.jamendo.com/track/1274490/stories

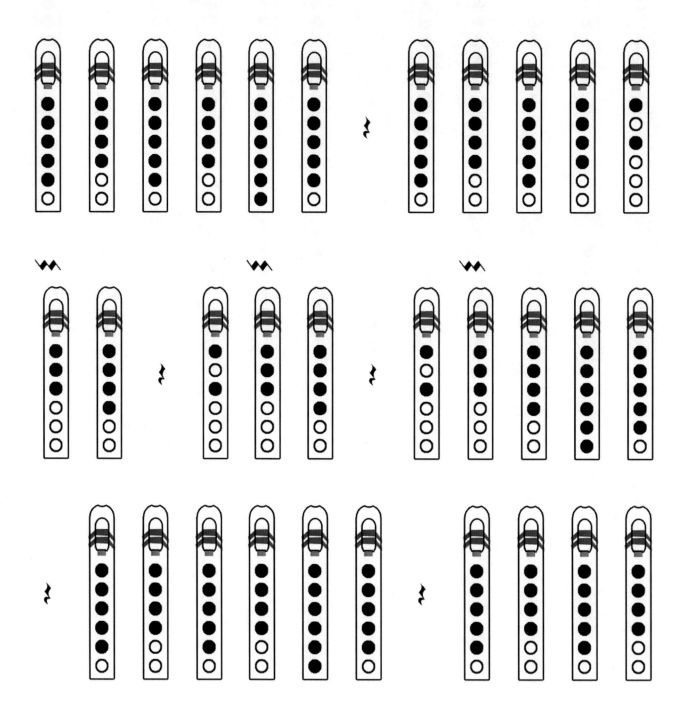

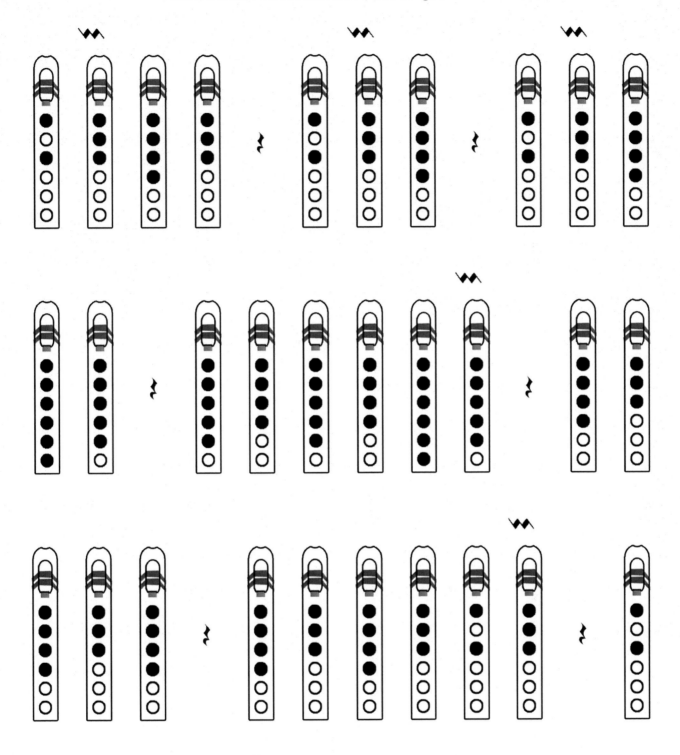

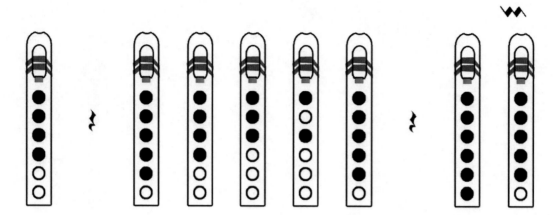

# Awakening

This is where the songs from "Awakening" album start. They are longer, usually between 3-4 minutes long.

This particular song, called "Awakening" (just like the whole album)) was composed for high-pitch flutes to be played in a fast, dynamic style.

Listen for free - https://www.jamendo.com/track/1290750/awakening-native-american-flute-solo

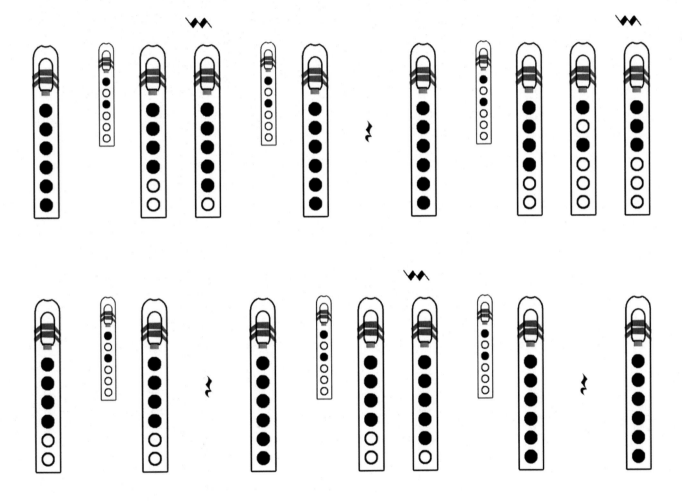

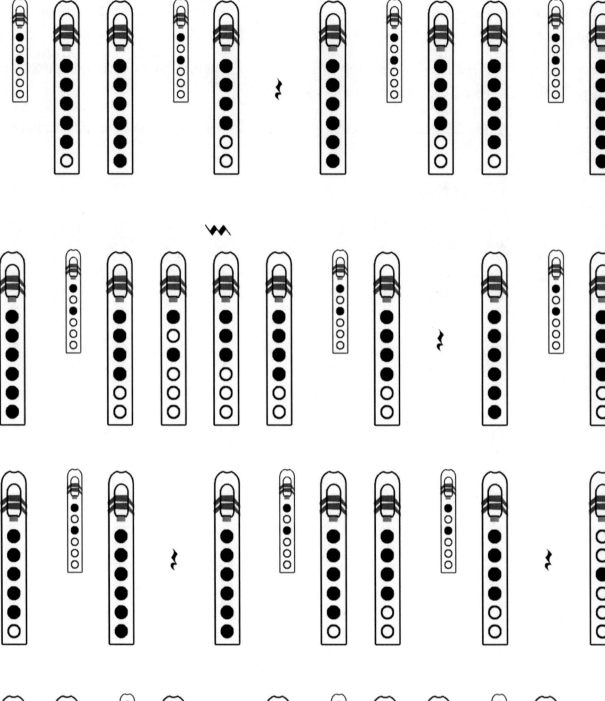

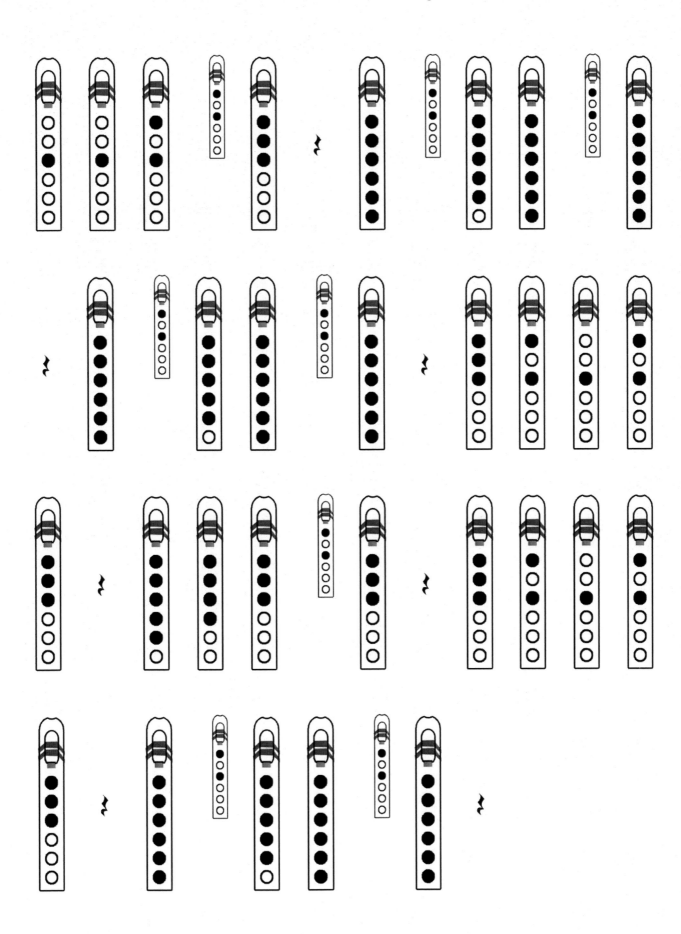

# Winds of Autumn

Listen for free - https://www.jamendo.com/track/1290751/winds-of-autumn-native-american-flute-solo

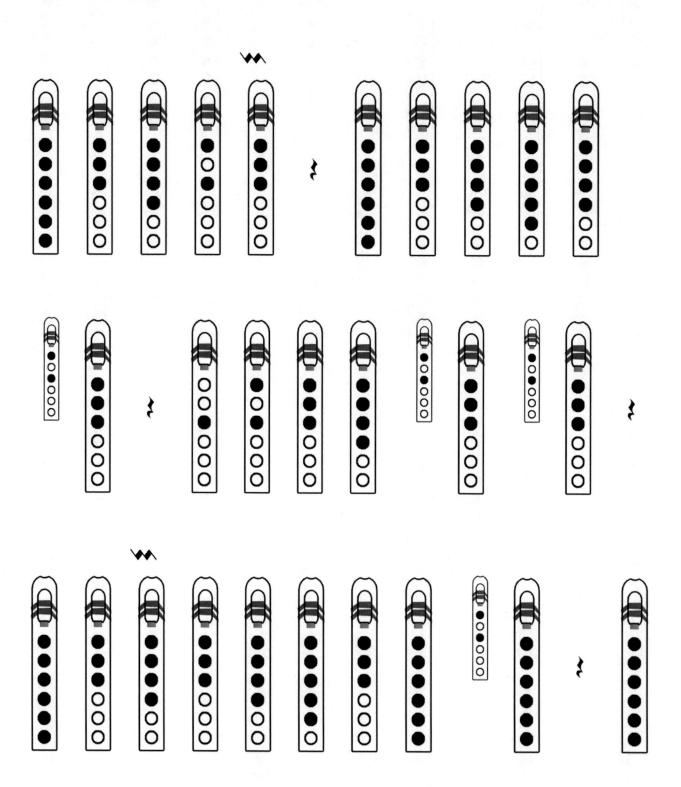

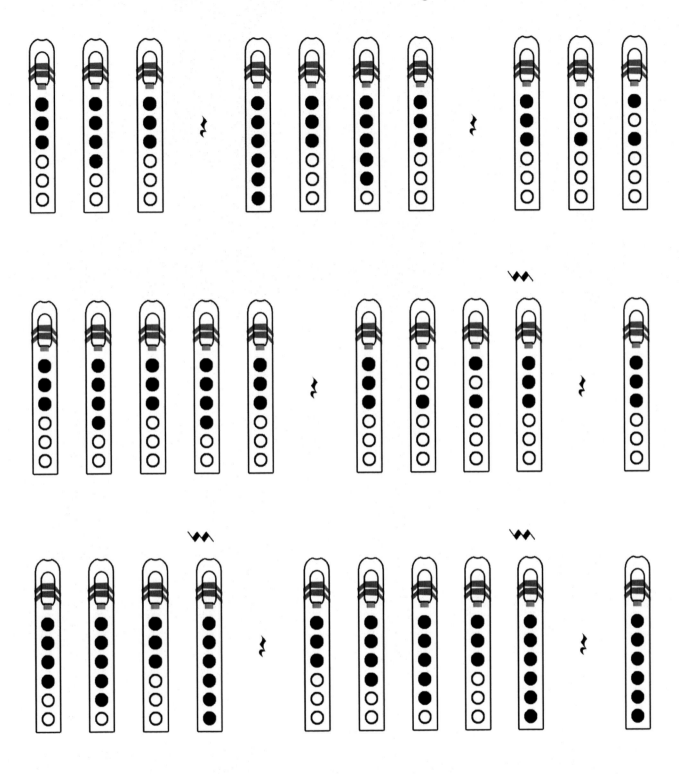

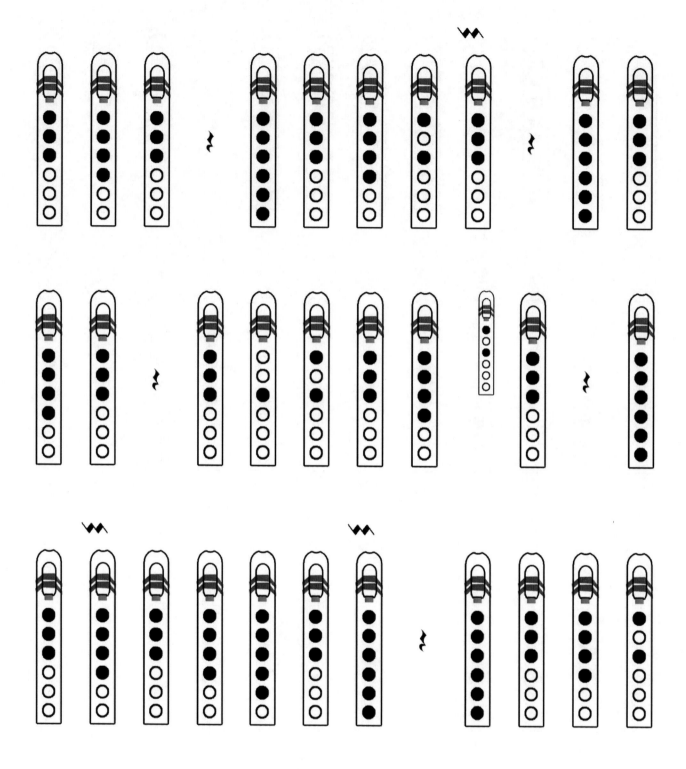

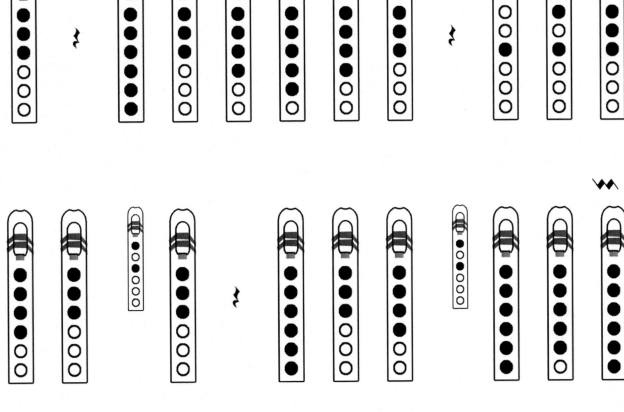

## Evening Song

Listen for free - https://www.jamendo.com/track/1290746/evening-song-native-american-flute-solo

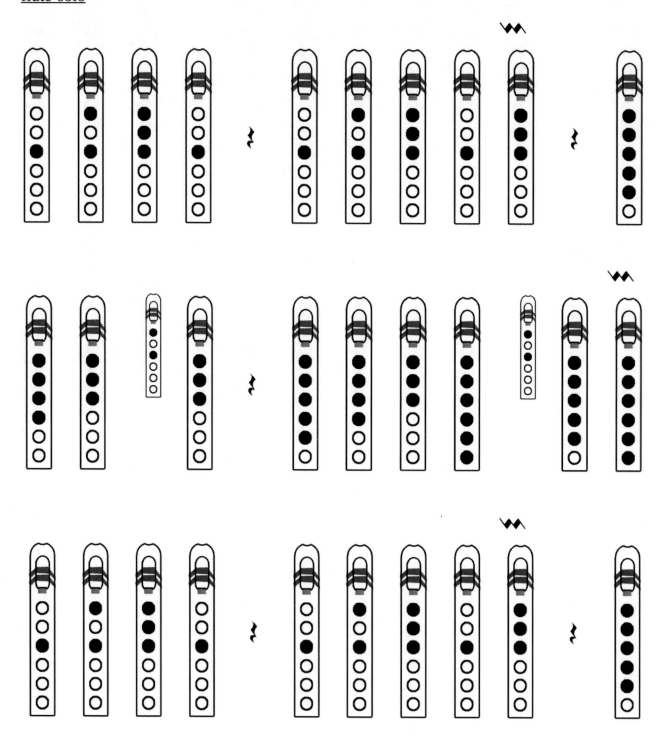

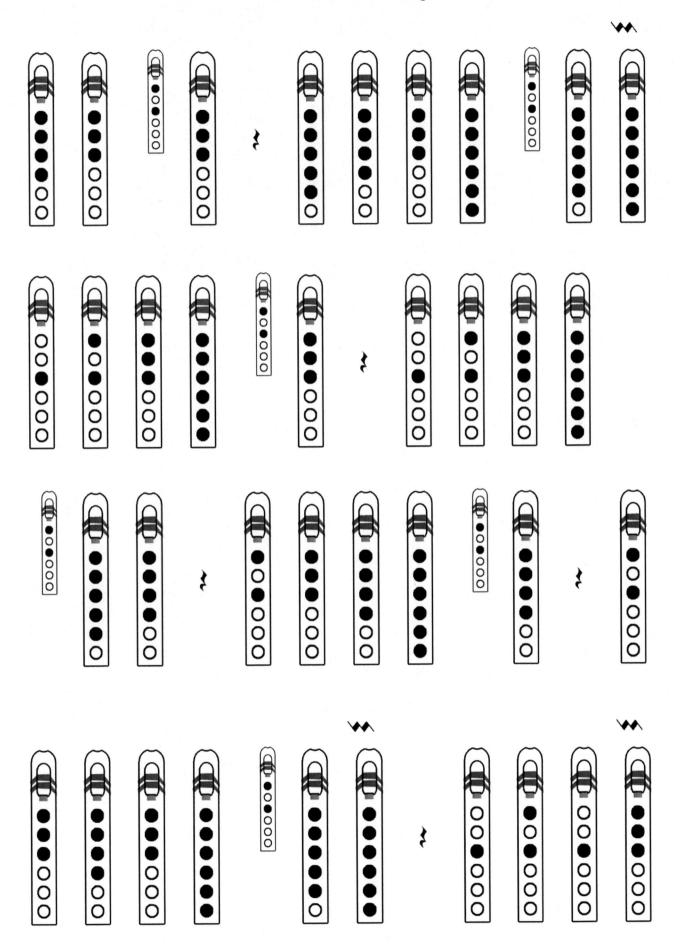

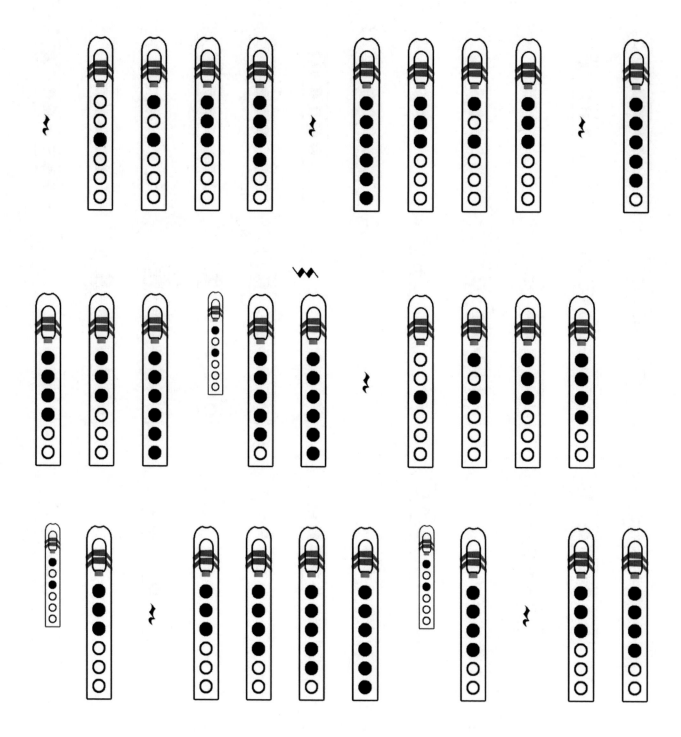

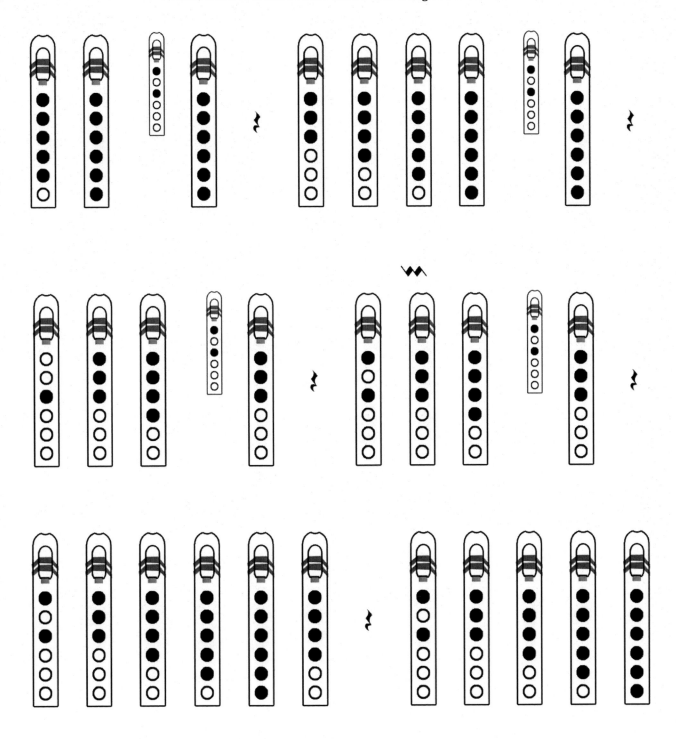

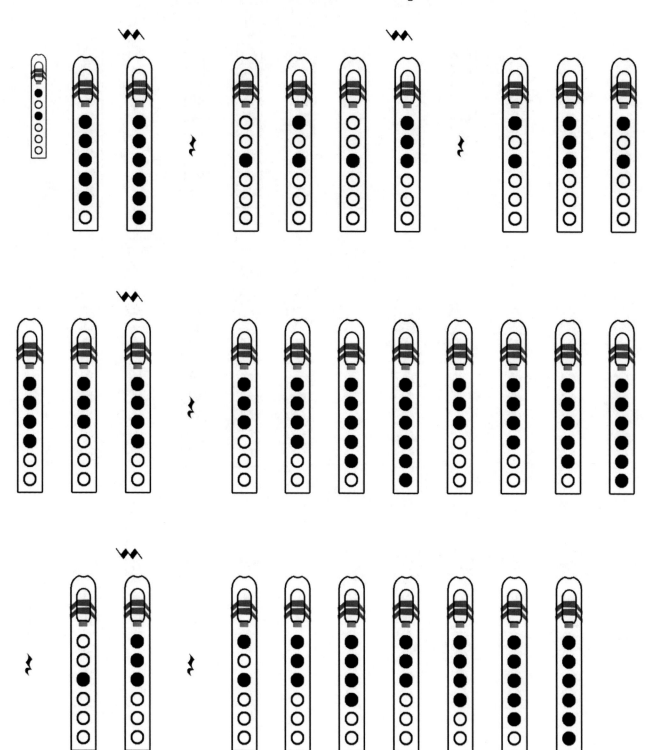

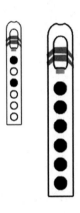

# Beauty

First 20 seconds inspired by morning song by Ronald Roybal and his Zuni sunrise song.

Listen for free - https://www.jamendo.com/track/1290745/beauty-native-american-flute-solo

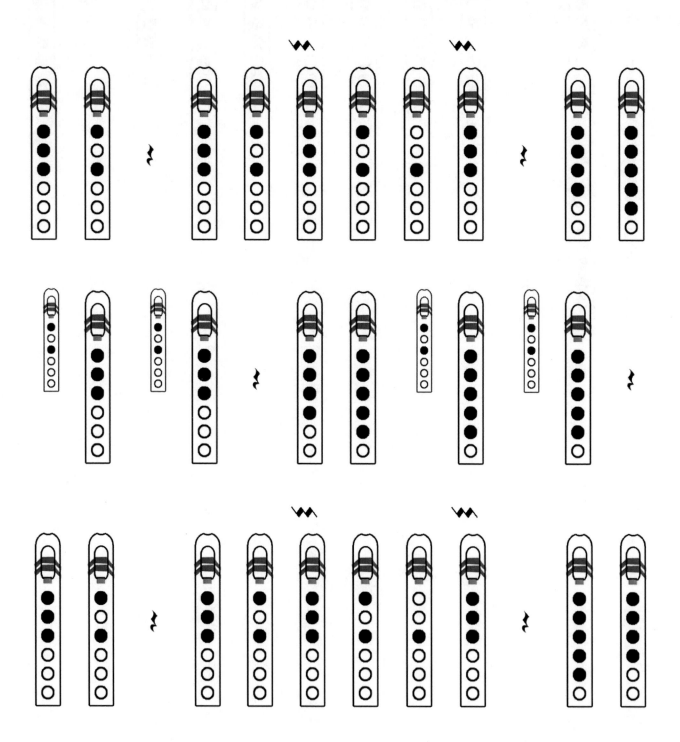

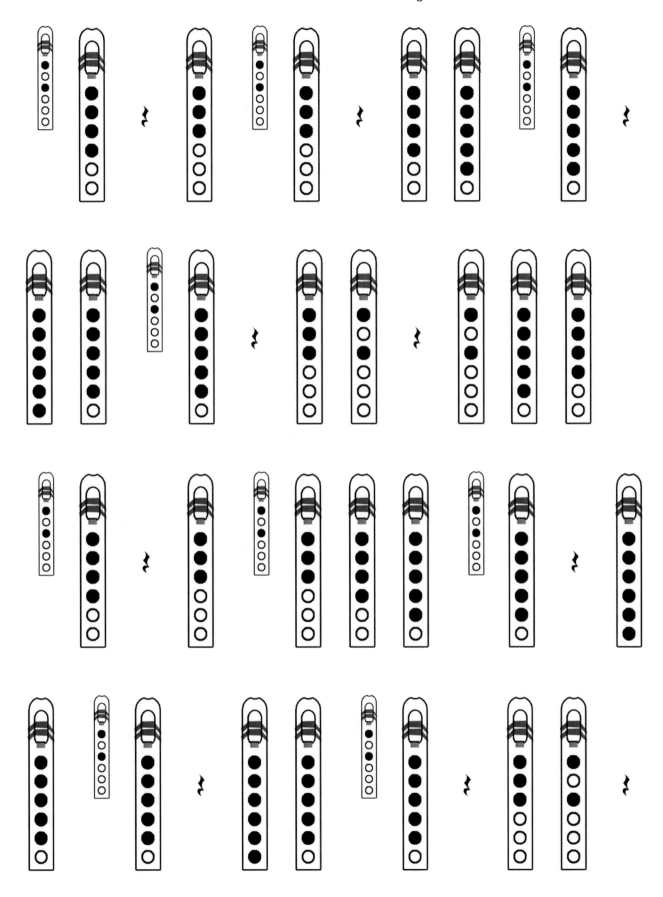

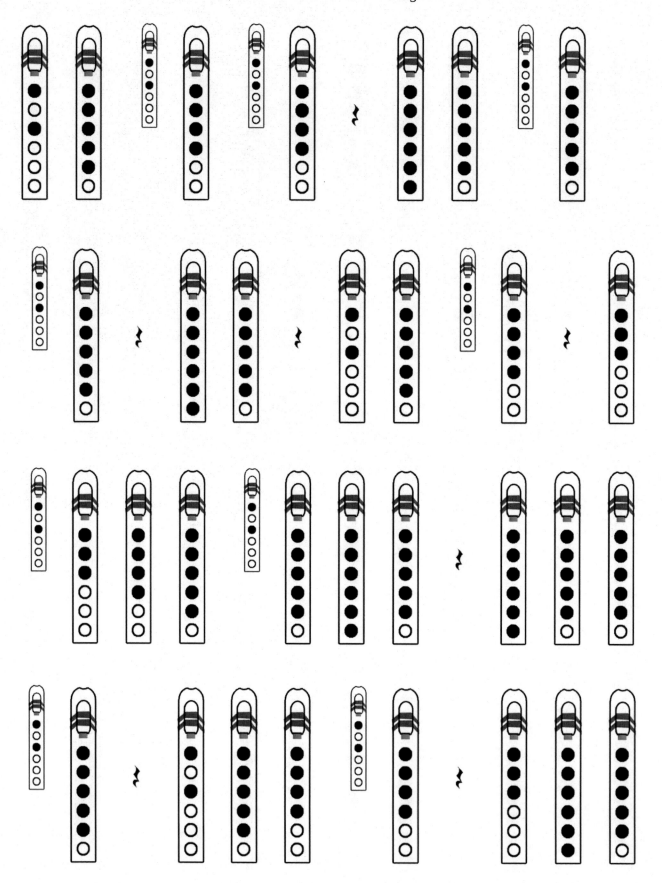

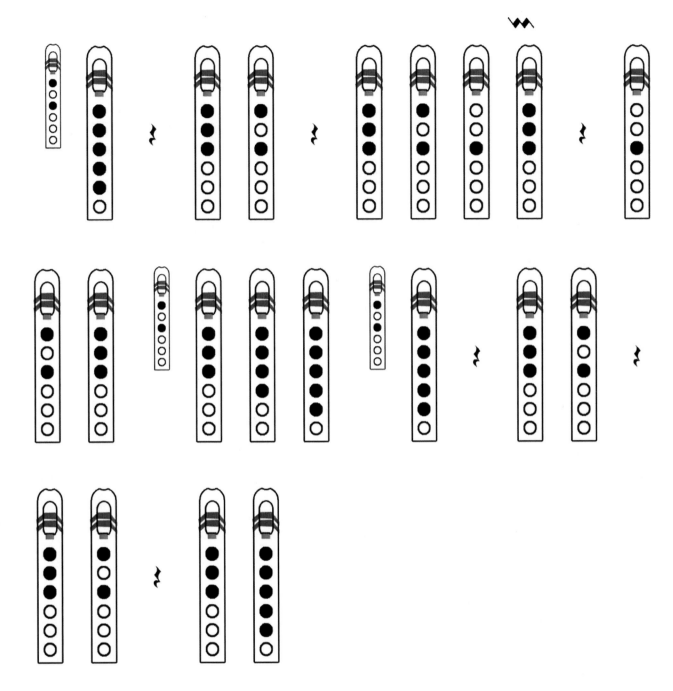

# Waiting

Listen for free - https://www.jamendo.com/track/1290755/waiting-native-american-flute-solo

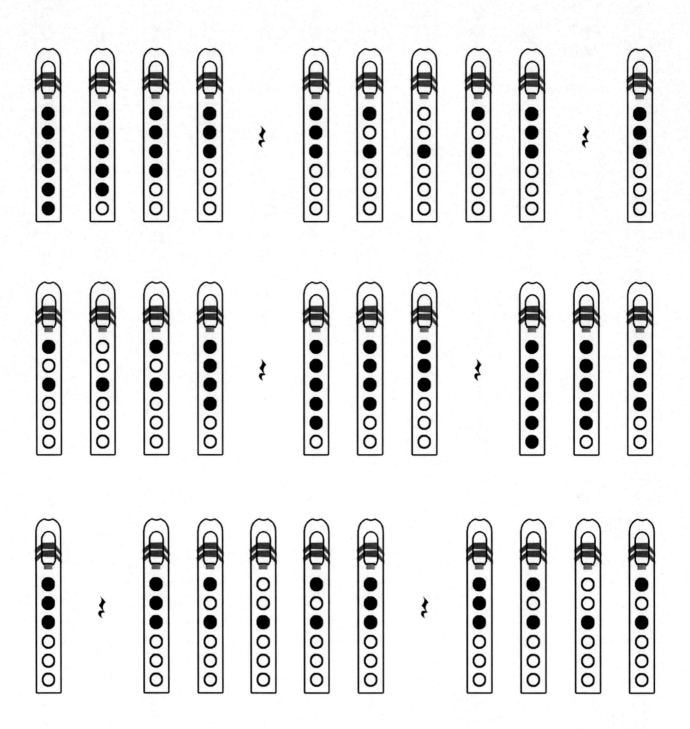

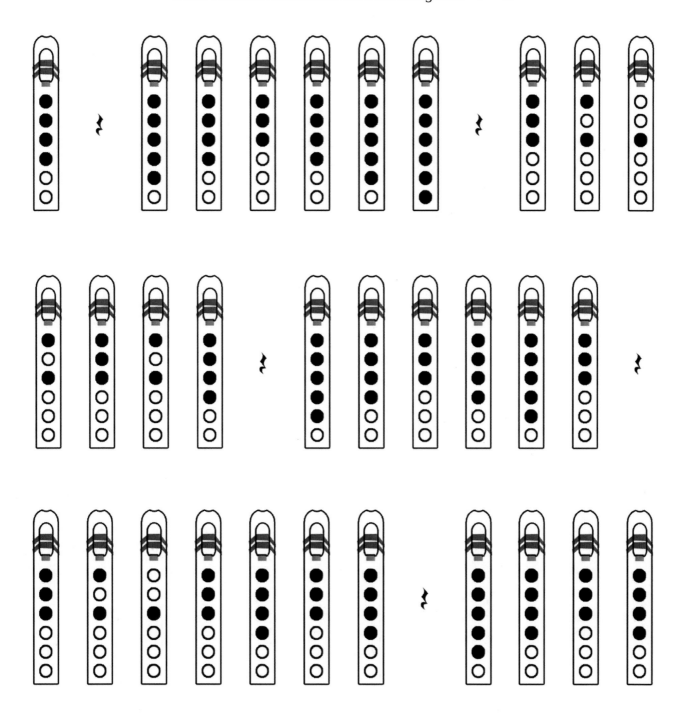

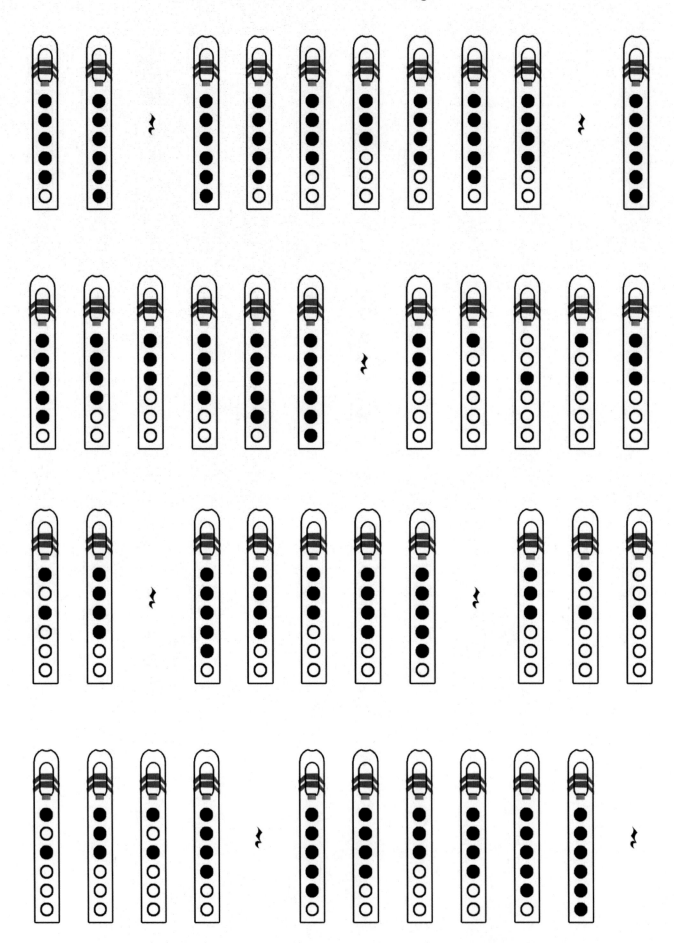

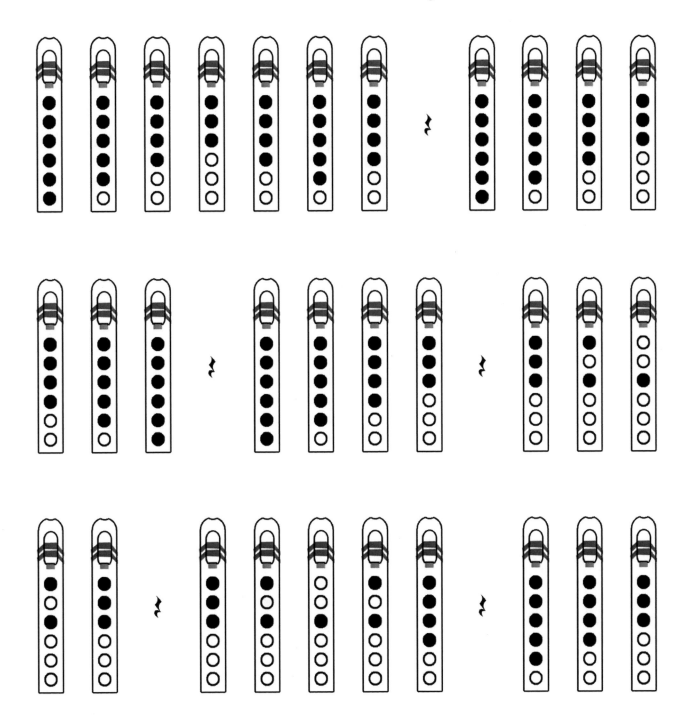

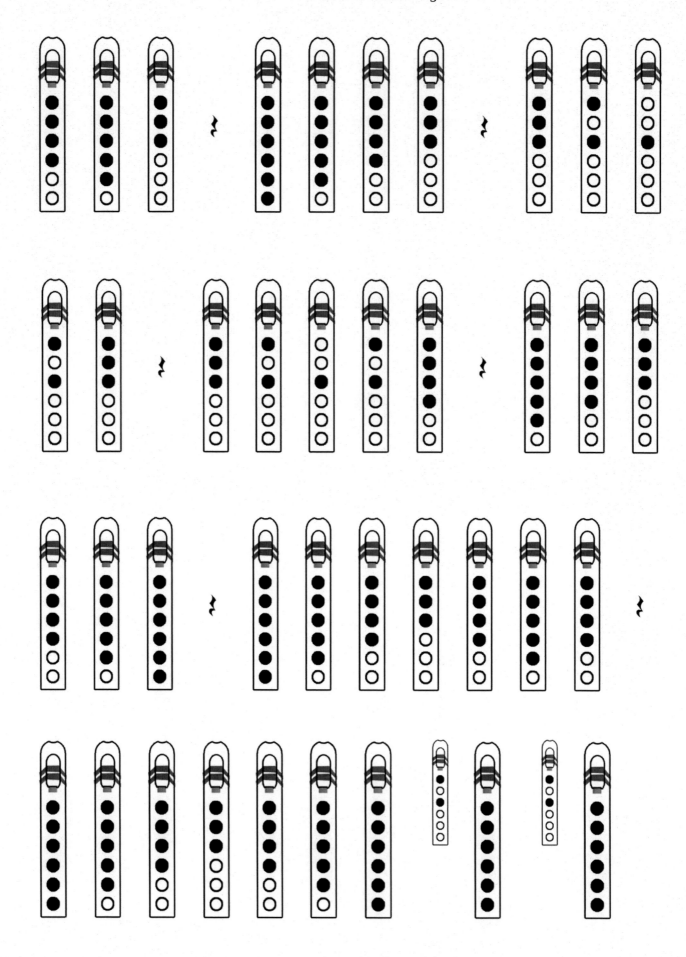

# Calling from Within

Listen for free - https://www.jamendo.com/track/1290747/calling-from-within-native-american-flute-solo

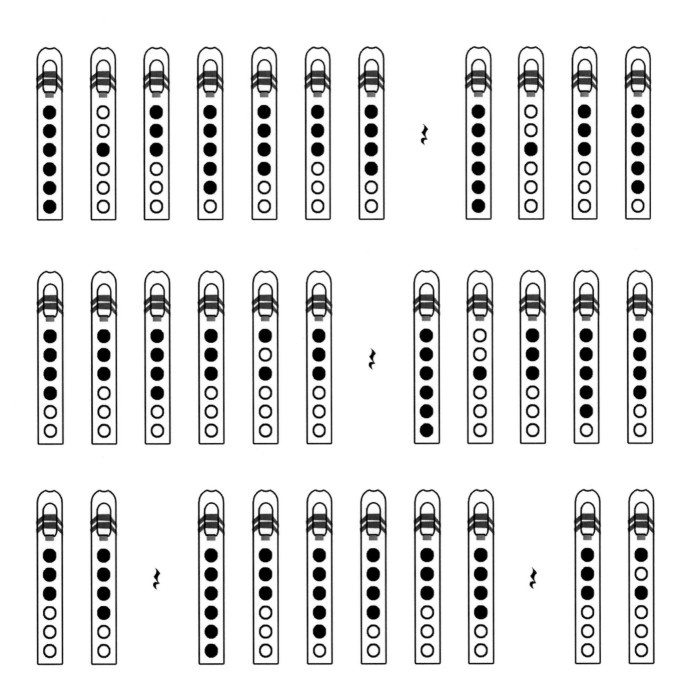

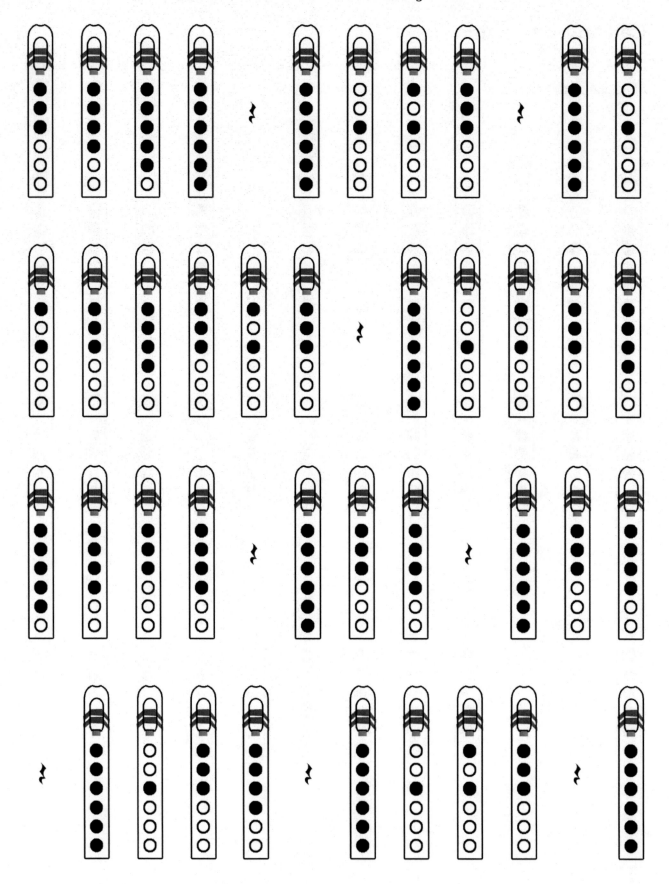

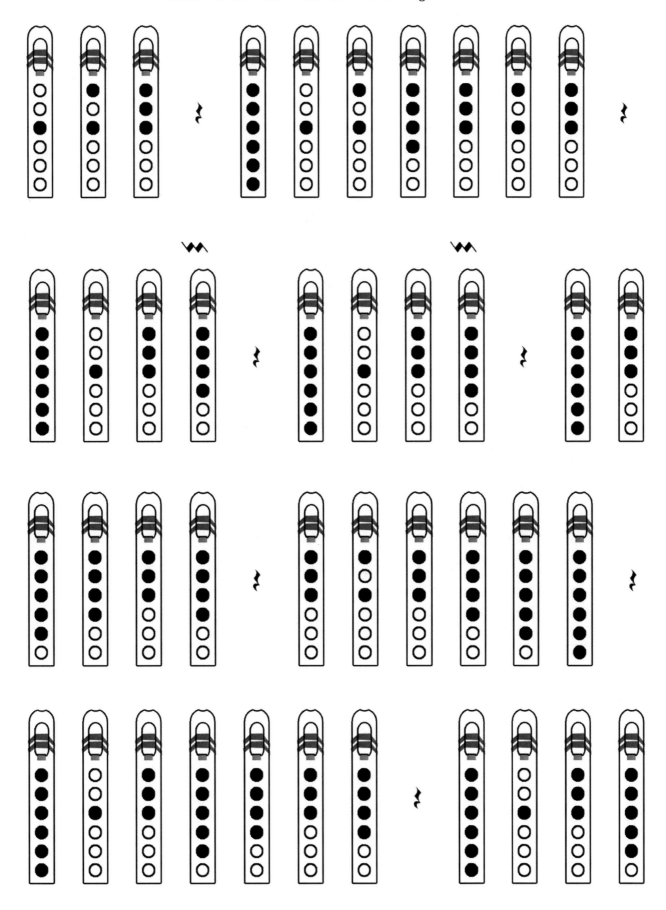

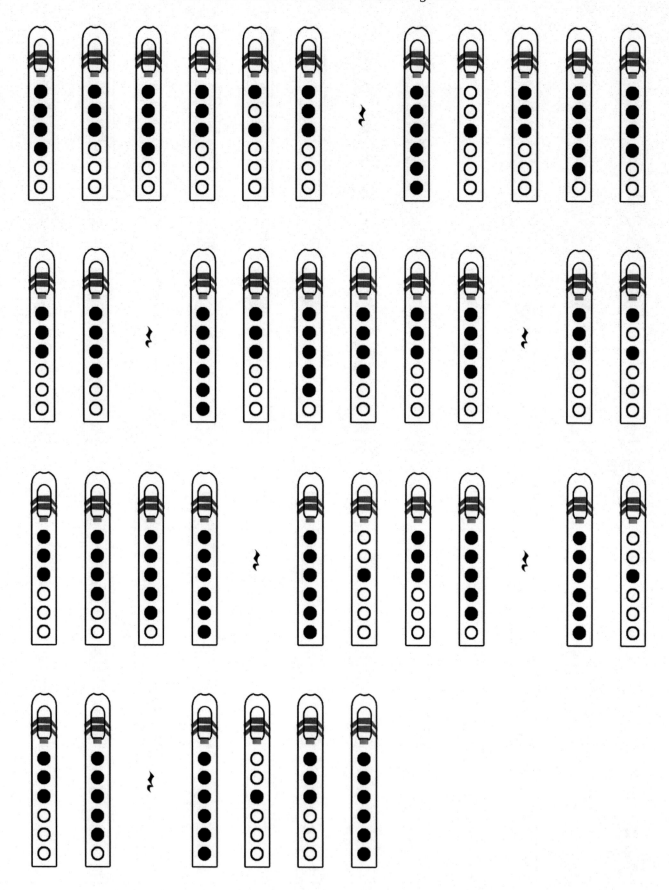

# Flowing

Listen for free - <u>https://www.jamendo.com/track/1290754/flowing-native-american-flute-solo</u>

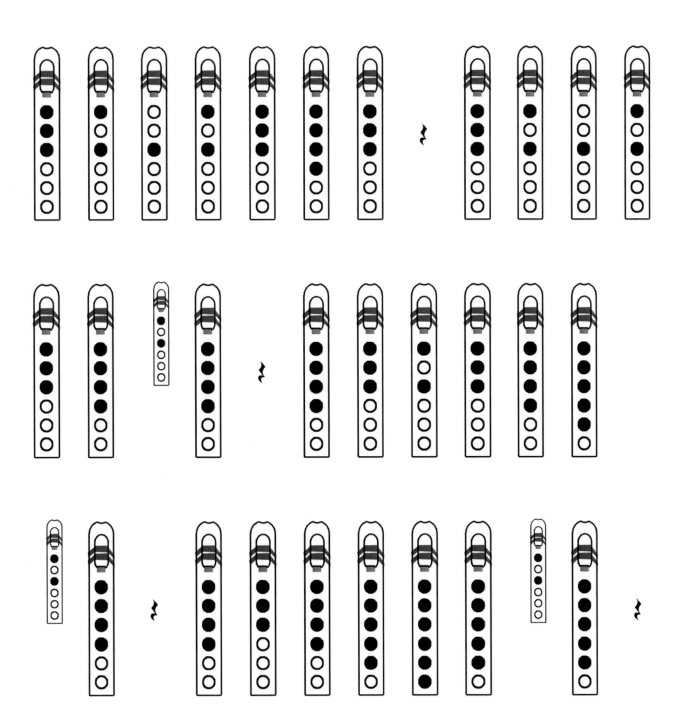

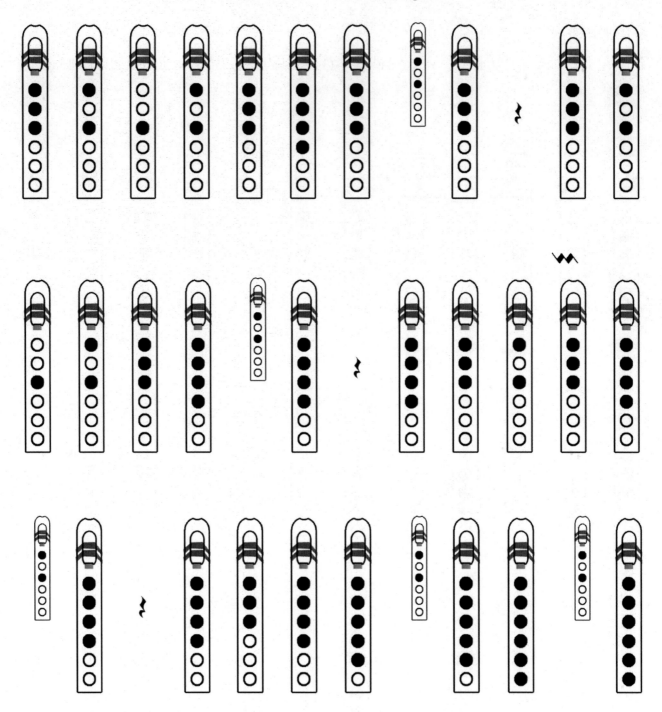

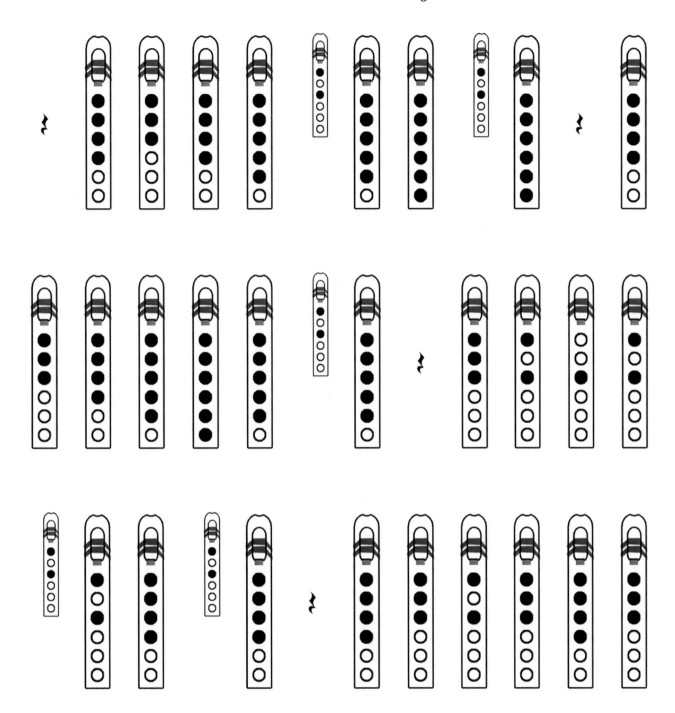

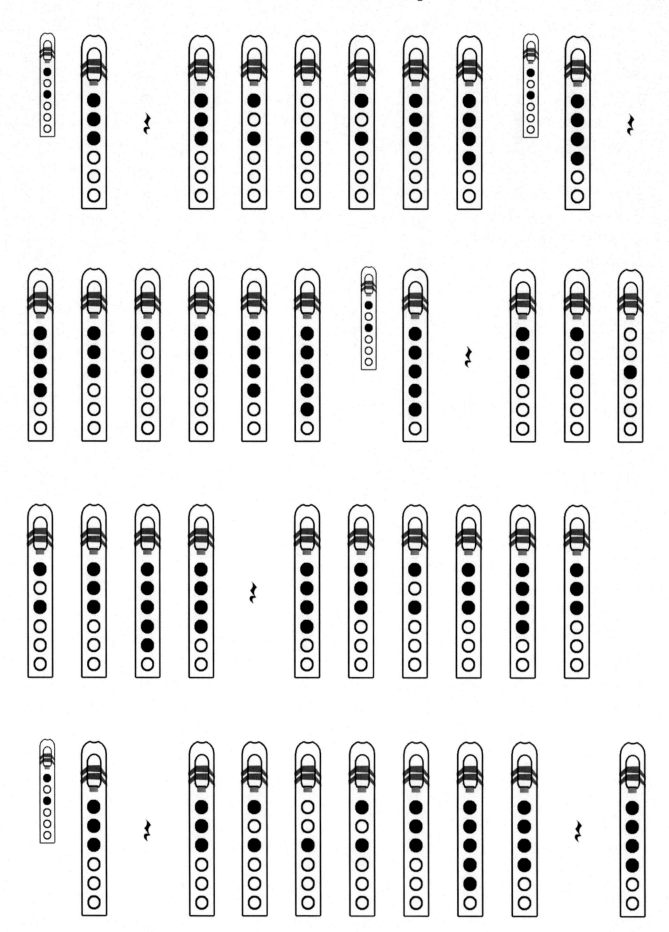

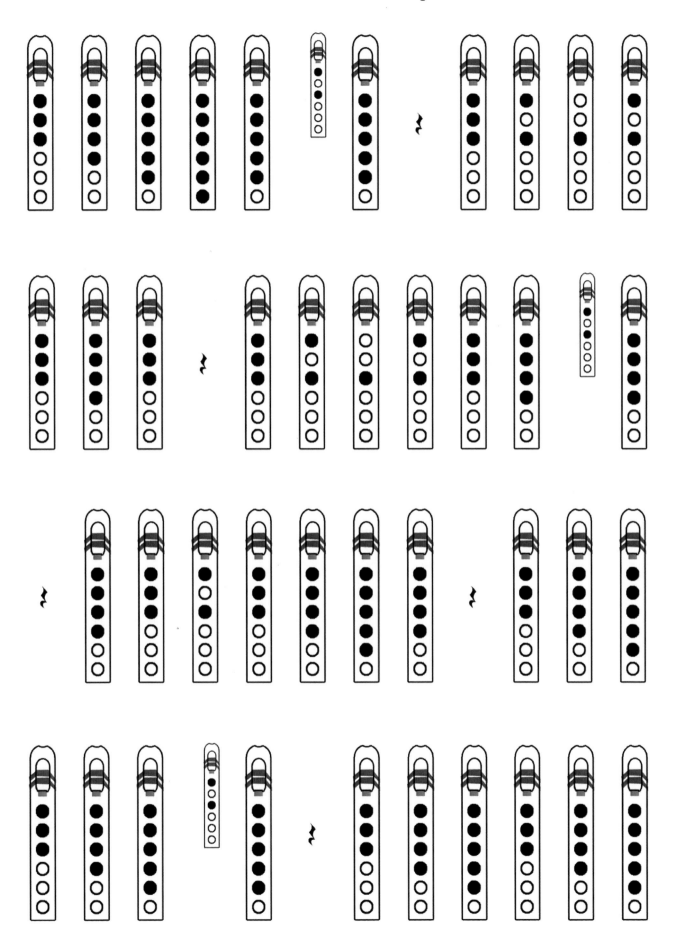

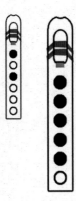

# Song of Five Spruce Trees

Listen for free - https://www.jamendo.com/track/1290728/song-of-five-spruce-trees-native-american-flute-solo

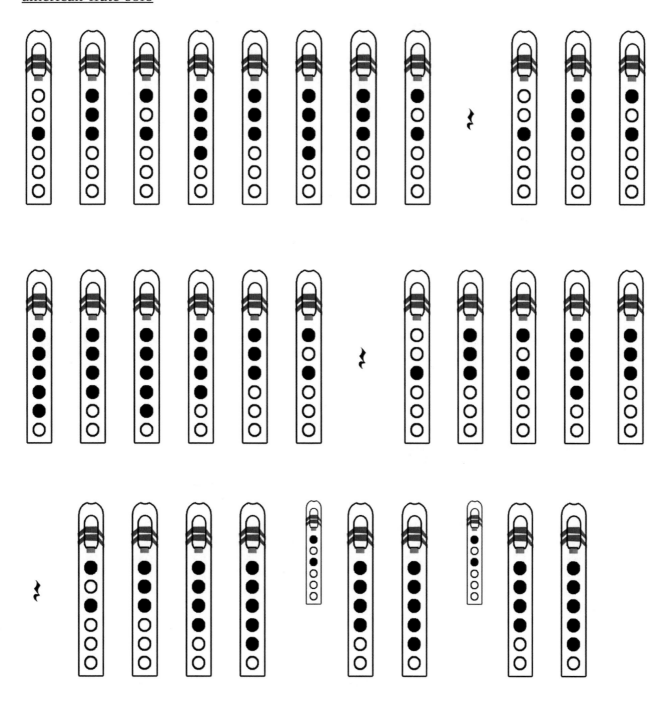

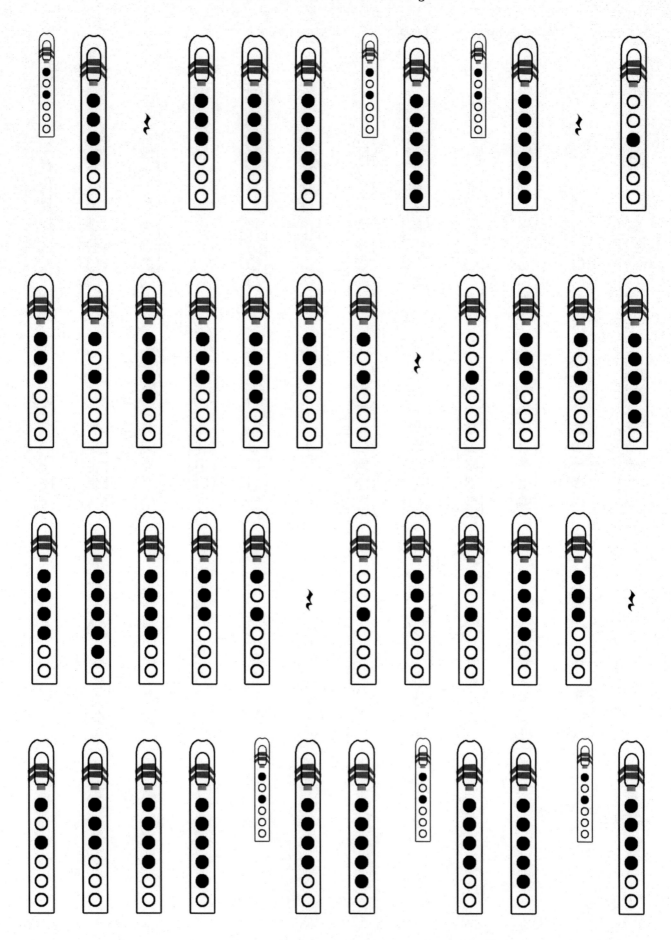

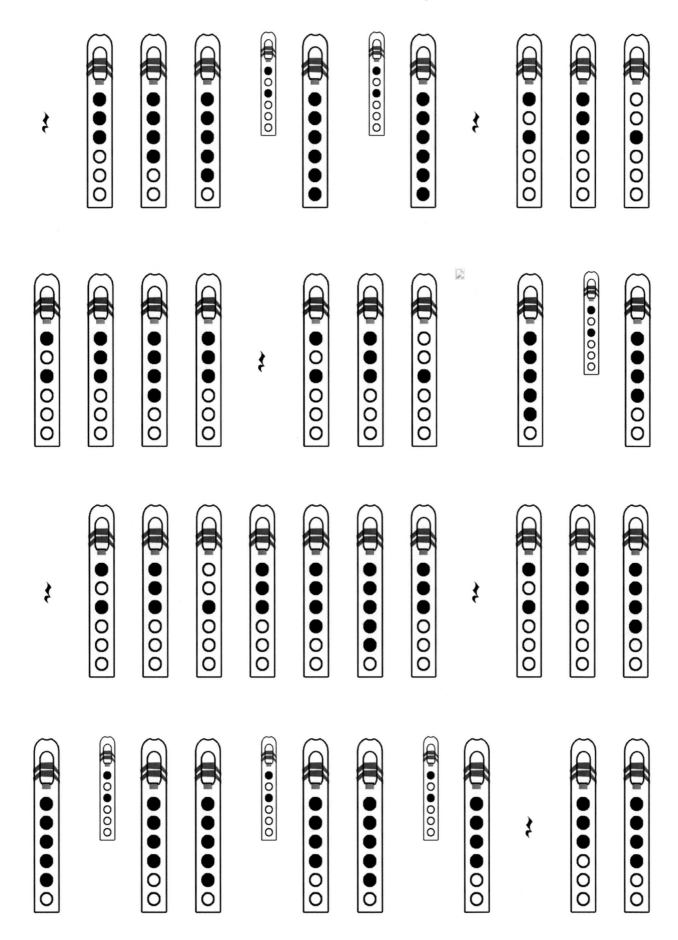

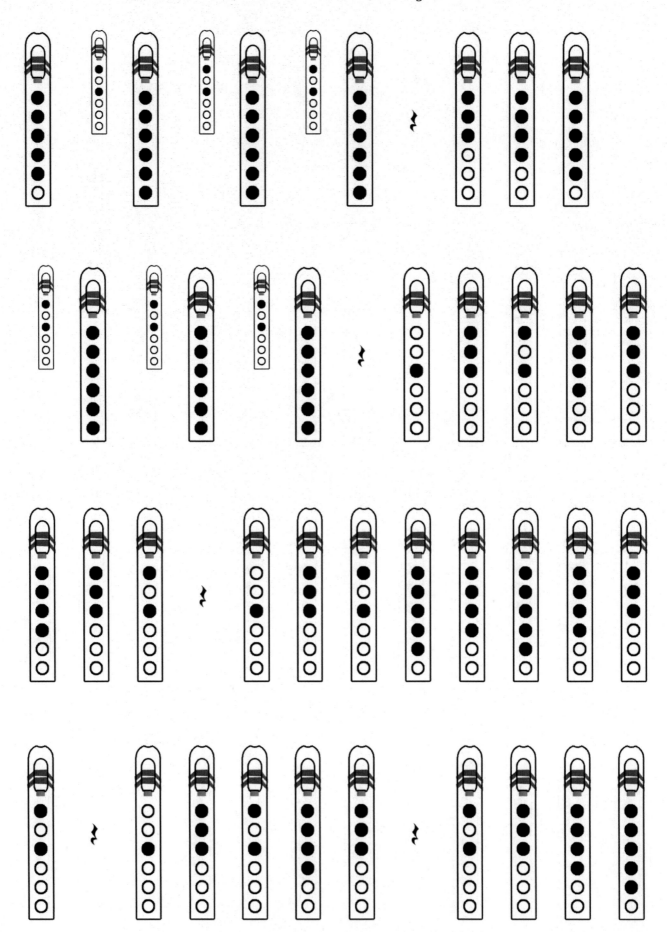

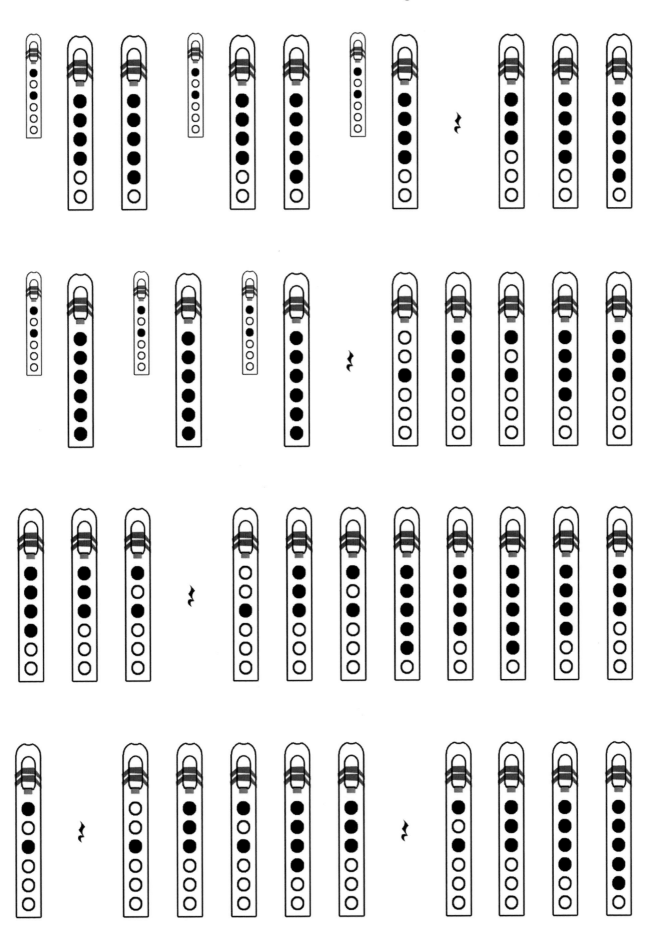

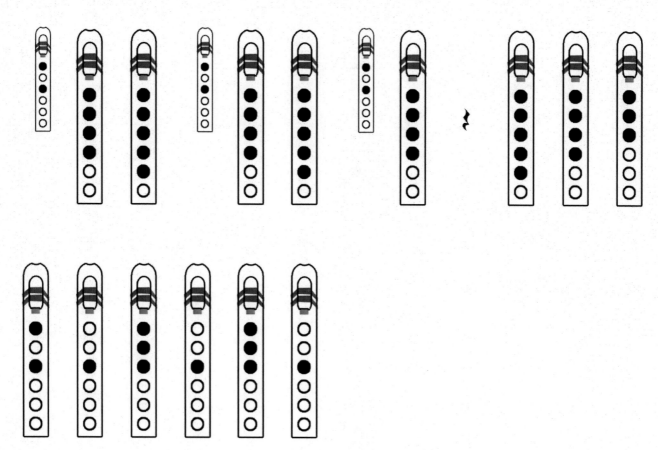

# Great Cities, Lonely People

Listen for free - https://www.jamendo.com/track/1290727/great-cities-lonely-people-native-american-flute-solo

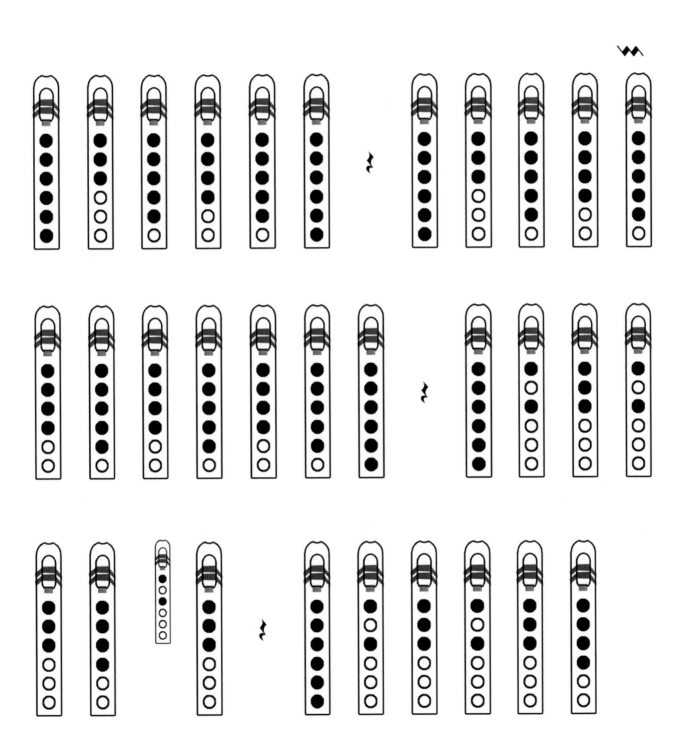

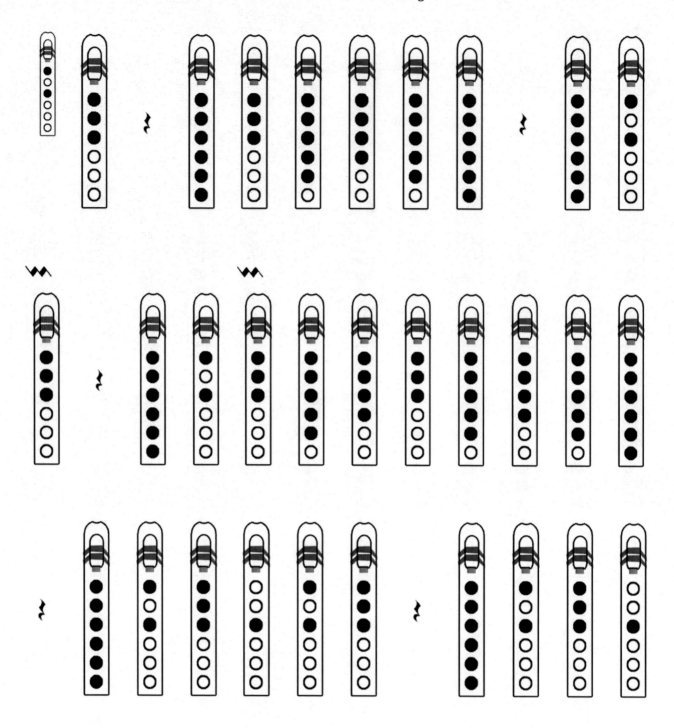

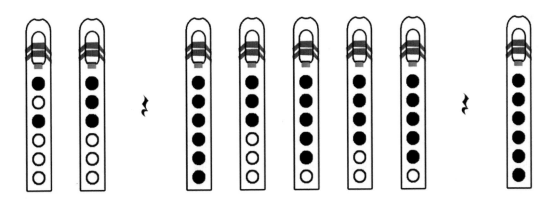

## New Day Will Come

Listen for free - https://www.jamendo.com/track/1290753/new-day-will-come-native-american-flute-solo

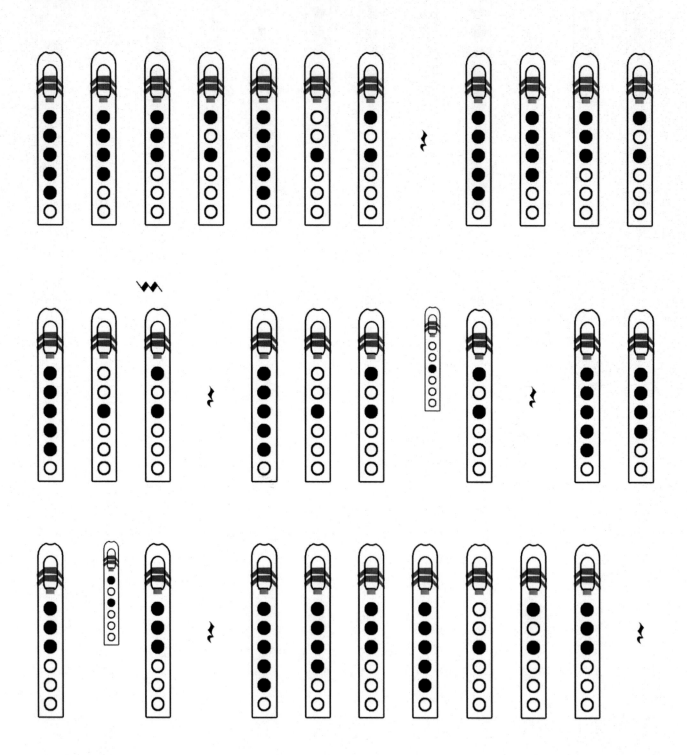

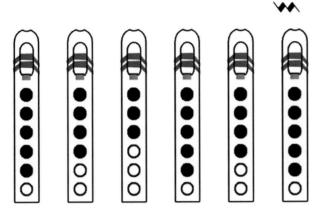

## Our Brothers, Our Sisters

Listen for free - https://www.jamendo.com/track/1290752/our-brothers-our-sisters-native-american-flute-solo

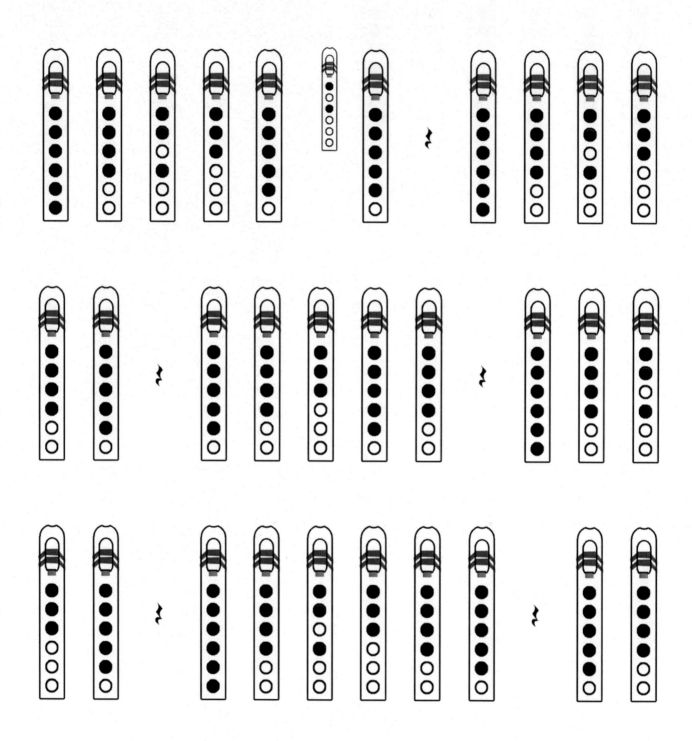

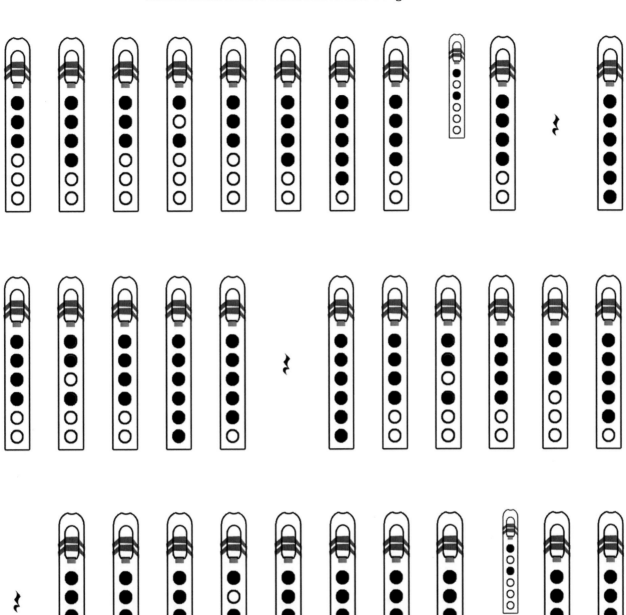

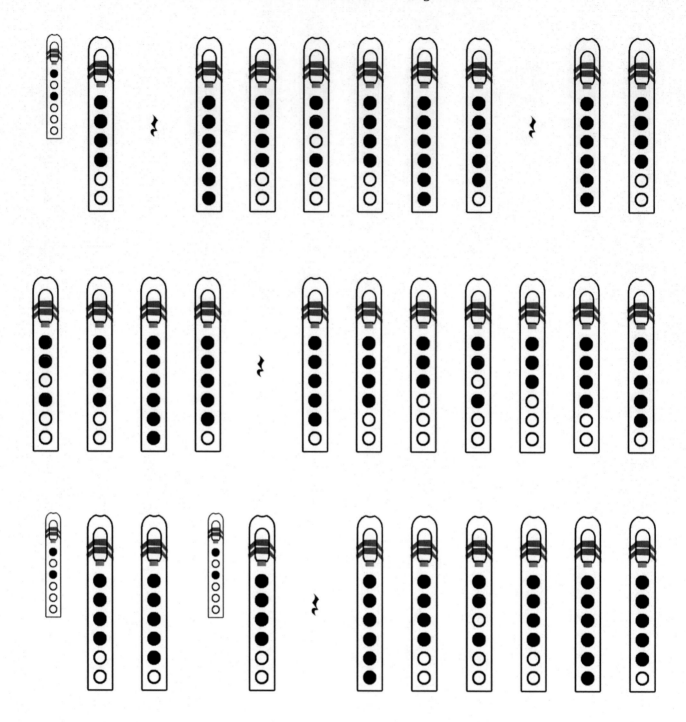

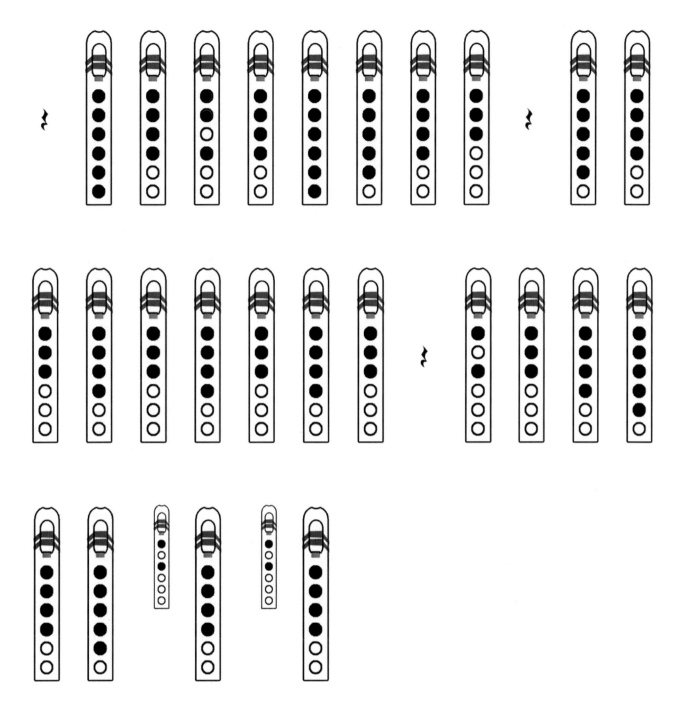

# Voices of the Mountain Spirits

Listen for free - https://www.jamendo.com/track/1290729/voices-of-the-mountain-spirits-native-american-flute-solo

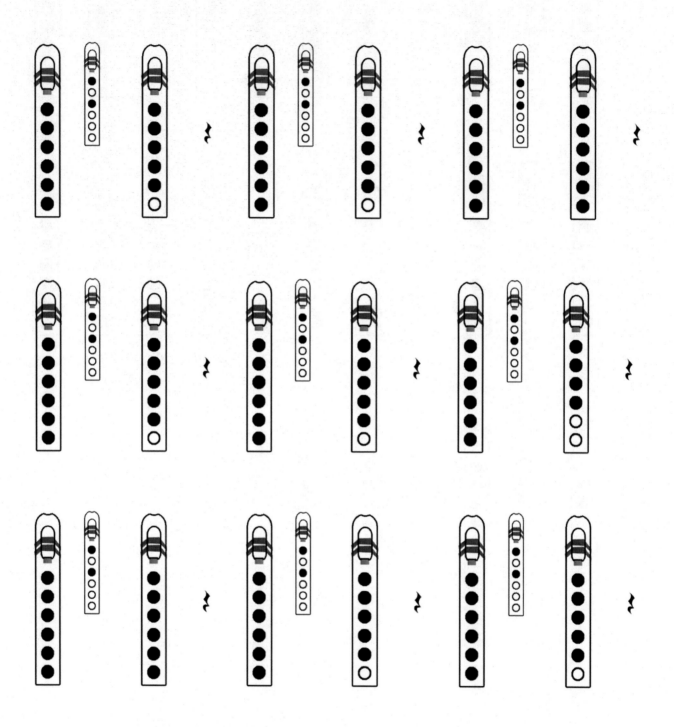

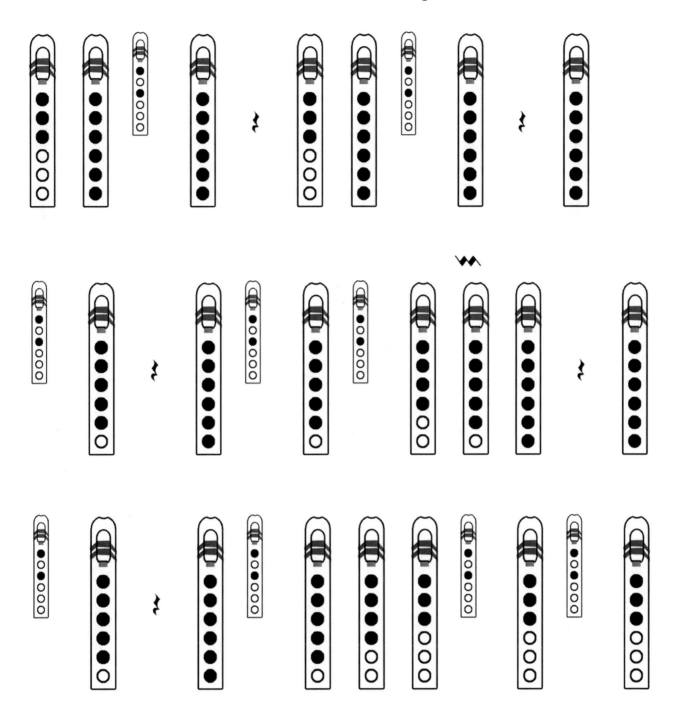

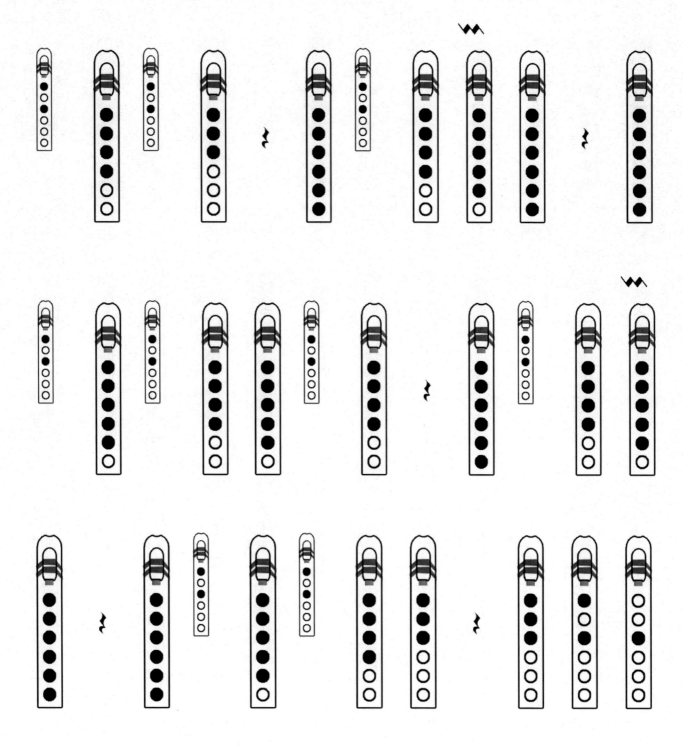

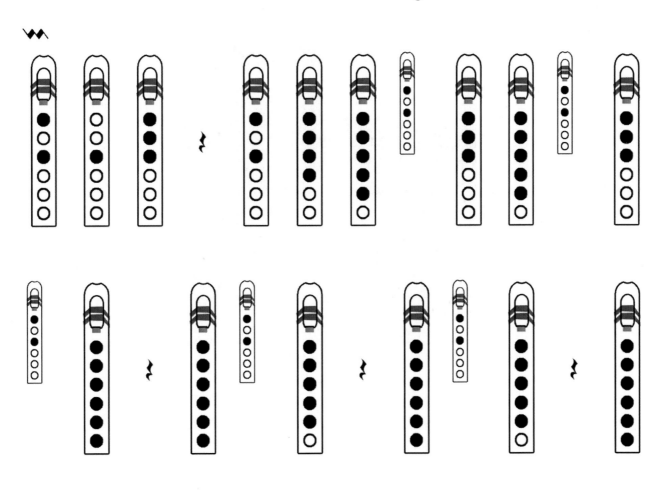

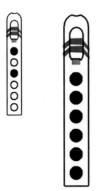

"Awakening" can be downloaded for **free** from Jamendo in "flute solo" version, as well as in "relaxation" version that includes sounds of nature in the background. If you need commercial licenses for YouTube, documentaries, games etc, you can purchase them through Jamendo, as well.

- https://www.jamendo.com/album/153742/awakening-native-american-flute-solo

- https://www.jamendo.com/album/147985/awakening

Made in United States
North Haven, CT
19 April 2024

51442568R00043